I0550122

EAST MEETS WEST

AMERICAN WRITERS REVIEW

SPRING 2015

Photo: Courtesy of Wendy Decker

East Meets West

American Writers Review

2015 Spring Edition

East Meets West American Writers Review 2015 Spring Edition

ISBN: 13-978-0-9905815-8-1

First published in the Unites States of America 2015

Copyright © Serenity Books Publishing, LLC

The Library of Congress has catalogued this book

The scanning, uploading and distribution of this book via the Internet or via any other means without the permission of the publisher is illegal and punishable by law. Please purchase only authorized electronic editions and do not participate in or encourage electronic piracy of copyrighted materials.

Publisher	Wendy Decker
Managing Editor	Patricia Florio/Co-founder
Cover Photo	Gerasimos Spathis
Interior Photos	Kevin Freibott
	Gerasimos Spathis
	Patricia Floiro

Judges:

Senior Judge	Ginger Marcinkowski
Fiction/Essays	Anne Henry
Poetry	Carol MacAllister
	Brian Fanelli

East Meets West

American Writers Review

The mission of East Meets West Writers Review is to provide a print journal for new and seasoned writers as a venue for their creative work.

Serenity Books is an independent book publisher founded by Wendy Decker, an award-winning writer and novelist. Wendy is also a member of the Society of Children's Book Writers and Illustrators and the Jersey Shore Writers based in Ocean Grove, NJ.

Patricia Florio, co-founded East Meets West American Writers Review with Sue Richter in 2010. Patricia and Sue, both writers writing for Striped Pot, an online travel e-zine started East Meets West as a writers' contest, but soon realized they wanted to Bridge the Gap between east coast writers and west coast writers, as well as, emerging and seasoned writers. The two published several EAST MEETS WEST journals and in 2014, Sue moved on to pursue new endeavors. Patricia teamed up Wendy Decker who recently launched the start-up publishing company Serenity Books Publishing, LLC.

East Meets West
American Writers Review

Congratulations to the authors of the Spring 2015 Contest

First Place: Lynne Spease Reader
                      Marked

Second Place: Rosemary Poole
                      Persephone

Third Place: D Ferrara
                      Sample Sale

Honorable Mentions

Nichole Kanney   The Bold and the Beautiful

Kayleigh Demace   Audrey

Finalists

Samantha Griffith   Our Last Dance

Gary Crawford   Encounter

Joel Heller   Butterfly

Staff Contributions

Brian Fanelli   Uncanny X-Men
                             Issues 141 and 142

Carol MacAllister   The Gift

TABLE OF CONTENTS

MARKED   Lynne Spease Reader   13

PERSEPHONE   Rosemary Poole   20

SAMPLE SALE   D Ferrara   29

THE BOLD AND THE BEAUTIFUL   Nichole Kanney   40

AUDREY   Kayleigh Demace   49

OUR LAST DANCE   Samantha Griffith   59

BUTTERFLY   Joel Heller   63

ENCOUNTER   Gary Crawford   65

UNCANNY X-MEN ISSUES
141 and 142   Brian Fanelli   74

THE GIFT   Carol MacAlliste   76

BRIDGING THE GAP - EDITOR'S DESK   Patricia Florio   78

AN ARTIST IN NEW ENGLAND   Annastaysia Jade Savage   82

CONFESSIONS OF A COURT REPORTER
(Excerpt)   Patricia Florio   89

SWEET TEA (Excerpt)   Wendy Lynn Decker   93

THE BUTTON LEGACY (Excerpt)   Ginger Marcinkowski   99

OUR STAFF   103

Prize Winners

East Meets West

American Writers Review

2015 Spring Edition

Photo: Courtesy of Gersimos Spathis

Lynne Spease Reeder

<u>Marked</u>

*T*he incessant hum of the tattooist's needle sent shivers through the lace fabric of the veil across my lap. I watched the way it shifted, tiny tremors from the earthquake happening upon my body. Across my left shoulder a graveyard garden blossomed. An exact replica of the veil, as it would have looked if I had been wearing it on my head like I was supposed to. Only instead of the innocent and lovely shade of white, the ink driving the memory forever onto my skin was harsh and unforgiving. Black as ashes.

"How you doin' there, sweetie?" the tattooist asked, his eyes never leaving the smeared edges of the stencil barely visible on my skin. He was a big guy, with a shaved head and gray mustache. He had a tattoo of a tarantula crawling up his neck.

Today was supposed to by my wedding day. I looked down at the wisp of material curling about itself like smoke across my legs,

13

forming the silhouettes of flowers plucked right from the Victorian era. I pictured a woman sitting in a plush-backed, red velvet chair. She would have had a veil like the one I held, straight from a time when women dreamt of romance and chivalry. I'd always dreamt of it too. I cleared my throat and clutched the scratchy swatch of lace tighter. "I'm fine, Steve. I told you, I'm sitting straight through."

"Tough chick," he said, and I could sense the approval in his voice. "I've had guys in here who couldn't stay still this long."

"Well," I sighed, "when you've felt pain like I have, this is nothin'."

Anyone else would have probably given me that god-awful look of confusion and pity. Steve wasn't one of those people, though. He re-inked his needle with a grunt, then looked at me for the briefest of seconds and said, "I hear that," and went back to outlining my sorrow.

It's funny how you miss the signs you're being tricked into believing happily ever after exists. How your whole life, older women are sure to tell you that fairy tales aren't real, that some things, like John, are too good to be true. It's funny how while it's all happening, they echo in your mind and you think you're the one who gets to break the rule. Then it happens, and you find yourself beside Steve instead of John, holding a veil instead of wearing it, covering yourself in black instead of white.

His funeral would have had to be a closed casket because of all the damage to his face, but it turned out we didn't have to worry about that because he'd wanted to be cremated. I hadn't known that; his mother told me. We'd only discussed the beginning of our life, not the end. I'd stood beside his family, not quite a part of them, at the memorial service, playing with the ring on my finger that was just a size too big but that I hadn't gotten resized, because I'd wanted this exact ring that he had put on my finger that night he'd pulled it from his pocket and looked at me. He'd looked at me. I'd stood there, in my black instead of white, thinking of the voicemail I'd listened to that morning letting me know my gown was ready to be picked up.

I looked down at my tattoo. It reached to the middle of my bicep, like a spider web I was catching myself in. I'd long since grown numb to the hot point of the needle, the way it felt more like slicing than jabbing. My heart felt a little lighter, like it had a partner in the crime of grief, another body part willing to carry the burden.

He'd been on his way to meet me to try wedding cake samples. I'd made an appointment to sample a selection from I Dough! Wedding Cakes and told John to meet me in the shop, even though it was a half hour drive from his work. I'd wanted him to taste the way the red velvet melted against your tongue, had pictured him leaning over with a partial laugh to wipe icing across my top lip, as if practicing for that indulgent moment of our reception where we'd feed each other. Perfect little Polaroid moment. Fairy tale pretty.

While listening to a doctor tell me over the phone why John was an hour late, it seemed odd to me that such a defining moment of my life was spent beneath a sign containing cheesy word puns and an oversized, personified cake. A knockoff of the Pillsbury Doughboy grinned at me while a gentle but impersonal voice chiseled through my happy ending with medical terminology that only translated to one thing: dead.

Tattooed across my mind, images of a tractor trailer moving too fast, an oversized grim reaper, turning and tilting and slamming into the man I never got to call husband. Glass breaking, hearts shattering, pictures burning around the edges.

The needle stopped, and the shop fell into a stunned type of silence. Steve wiped down my arm and while he wrapped it up with plastic wrap, making me think of packing sandwiches for lunch, he explained to me how to care for this over the next few days. The veil was beginning to itch my leg, the lace suddenly scratchy and overdone. Who was I kidding? I wasn't sure people even really wore veils anymore. They were the stuff of fairy tales.

I walked to the mirror strapped beside the cash register. I finally looked how I felt: marked. I didn't look like some girl wasting her time wishing on stars. I looked like life had slapped me.

After I'd paid and left Steve a hefty tip, I walked out the door and down the sidewalk. I let the wind snake the veil from my hands, and I didn't even turn to watch it twist away from me.

"Oh, wait! Excuse me! Miss?" A young girl came running up behind me and grabbed my elbow. When I turned around, she had the veil in her hand. Her eyes were kind and her hands were soft. "I think you dropped this. It's beautiful, by the way."

I saw the ring on her left hand, the tiny diamond. Just one of them. No wedding band yet. I smiled at her, aware of the ache in my left shoulder. "Keep it."

She looked confused. "What?"

"I don't need it anymore." I looked ahead of me, at the bench that reminded me of where John had proposed, the bagel shop that reminded me of how he liked the ones with poppy seeds, the American flag on a storefront that reminded me of the miniature ones flapping beside some of the gravestones leading up to John's.

I looked back to this girl, with her big eyes and unbroken heart. "Consider it your something borrowed," I told her.

And as I walked away, I smiled for the first time in months. I looked like life had slapped me but I'd found a way to make the scar beautiful.

John would have loved the look on that girl's face.

Bio – Lynne Spease Reeder

Lynne Reeder earned her MA in Creative Writing from Wilkes University. She resides in her Pennsylvanian childhood hometown with her high school sweetheart and brilliantly independent daughter, and draws inspiration from the many people and experiences she's had. Lynne spends her days valiantly trying to pass along her lifelong passion for reading and writing to her secondary English and creative writing students, where every now and then great life truths make themselves known--which is what reading and writing are really about, in the end.

Photo: Courtesy of Kevin Freibott

Second Place Winner

Rosemary Poole

Persephone

PERSEPHONE is the goddess queen of the underworld, wife of the god Haides. She is also the goddess of spring growth, who was once worshipped alongside her mother Demeter in the Eleusinian Mysteries. This agricultural-based cult promised its initiates passage to a blessed afterlife.

Persephone: The Unspeakable Girl

1.

Last October's corn, tooth-hard and wrinkled,

is buried in the iron of December.

The germ of the new crop, it will make

a pale green and glistening arrival

in April's opening light.

Spring will pierce the ice at last.

But for a moment, the seed

lies still, an open space

into which something will grow.

It's while the germ lies quiescent

that the formidable dead raise their voices

to speak in the present tense.

They circle the living waving their boney arms,

and whisper words no one wants to hear.

Rasping laments echo

through limbo's chamber, threaten

to shake the present into rubble,

to stunt the growth of grain

and shrivel the blossoming olive.

But there lives a paradox in mortals:

they are containers for the past and the dead

and out of those containers spring

the hours and days of their actions:

their lives. This baffling capacity

to be living and dead and

the motion between:

fixed and moving,

flesh and fleeting light,

contradiction and harmony --

this power is like a god.

This god absorbs words like black rock

absorbs heat. She soaks up curses,

betrayals, failures and regret

and in the furrows of her enveloping

robes, she transforms them

into bleating lambs; unfolding buds;

the flood of life rushing into itself.

Because she is sound and silence, both,

language cannot contain her,

and her name must never be spoken.

She is called the Unspeakable Girl.

II.

<u>The Girl As Seen</u>

I ran across a girl picking flowers

on a hillside, afloat with her playmates,

her slight body wiry,

her quick eyes glancing,

testing the depths of the canyon.

She'd lived long in childhood's sleeve --

the yellow dress and the poppies,

her mother's anxious breathing.

How long before the chafe,

the surge of her pulse would bewilder

her thighs -- the cool, dark shade

would invite her?

As I watched she began to bend

away from her friends, so familiar

she hardly knew where she began

and they ended. I saw her pause at a pool

in a glade of aspen to ponder

for the first time her own reflection --

the gold and white of her hair --

the wavering pink of her face.

Sighing, she raised her head.

And in that moment she flushed

with the pungent air of the hidden

and the dark's rich scent.

She glanced once back at the pasture --

misty girls, naiads in the grasses.

But beside her the sky crashed earthward,

and the mouth of the dark opened up.

She bent herself willing toward night,

the cold cold thrum of desire --

and was gone.

III.

<u>Demeter: The Blindness of Loss</u>

Demeter is like a well.

A bucket lowered into her spring

will carry sweet water to the surface.

But she is not the water

formed in the earth's core.

She is the breach in the crust,

and through her the water rises.

When she discovered her child was gone

she threw off her goddess robes

and wandered in dismal grief

like any mortal woman.

Not as a traveler would, setting her foot

on the door sills of strangers or striding

bold to the unknown, exploring. No.

Shod with the lead of her unburied loss,

weighted down by her emptied heart,

everywhere she sought her girl.

But she begged for her springtime daughter

to no avail.

For Demeter searched for a girl.

She never thought to look

for a goddess.

Bio

Rosemary Poole

R. W. Poole lives in New Hampshire where she spends most of her days thinking about myths and stories and how humans use them, and most of her mornings writing poetry. She is currently compiling a chapbook focused on the myth of Persephone.

Photo: Courtesy of Gerasimos Spathis

Third Place Winner

D Ferrara

<u>Sample Sale</u>

*B*randi loved clothes. More than wine spritzers, more than summer. Not just any clothes - designer names. Clothes with three and four place price tags. Clothes that she couldn't afford, that cost more than her car (when she had a car). Maybe not more than she had loved her mother – but her mother was dead, leaving a piddling life insurance policy, a smaller bank account, a sense of how to pull together a drop dead look and little else.

Moving to a studio, Brandi sold her mother's wardrobe and let the car be repossessed. She had dropped out of junior college when her boyfriend was drafted and sent to Germany (at least it wasn't Vietnam) and switched to full time at Nirvana. In other words: first Nordstrom's, then Neiman Marcus.

These stores wanted their floor personnel to dress well. While the clothes weren't free, there were employee discounts. Special clearances. Mismatched sizes. End of run. All painlessly charged to the house account. The wealth of a shop girl was not reflected in her paycheck (small and eroded further by required payments to the store). The riches crammed in the closet, piled on the dresser, the vanity, the bathroom: Silk. Rayon. Microfiber. Cashmere pillowing on the couch. Wool blends, firmly knit, or loopy. Treasures beyond the imagination of those shoppers relegated to Macy's - or worse.

Merely owning these clothes paled after the first wearing. Cloaked with the invincibility only haute couture could impart, standing at the mirror (itself hung with yesterday's treasures), the fortunate one assumed super heroine stature, beyond mere wearers of garments. Crowned, gowned and dazzling, the diamante diva was more than mortal. The rush could last all day. Brandi wished that she could rekindle the thrill a second time, but once worn, the magic fled. Her armor became mere clothes, then upholstery or floor coverings.

Even better than the discounts were the secret treats. Junior buyers, anxious to solidify their positions would seek out their favorite salesgirls, thrust an extra this or that. "A shrug," they'd explain. "Not a shawl. Sort of a sweater, but more luxe." Wisps of color barely knotted together. No one would snap a credit card for such a thing on a hanger, but as mauve filament wrapping size two shoulders, the shrug would become desirable, even necessary.

"Must have" was the ultimate status. A must-have had the power to render a second wearing tolerable (if only as a matter of duty). Finding a must-have could catapult a junior buyer to senior, a senior to management. Wearing a must-have could increase a salesgirl's commission until it almost covered the debt she had built up.

That was why she left Neiman. Nordstrom's had been her first foray into high fashion. She had left Nordie's for Neiman's more generous discount (and more expensive clothes). Neiman's was Wonderland until accounting told her she owed the store more than she would earn in months. Stripped of the privilege of buying, work was merely drudgery. After that, she determined, it was better to work in an office for more money.

She found an office job in the city, quickly, though not in an elegant glass tower. On the edge of fashionable quarters, in a building leaning into disreputable, she interviewed with a man more interested in her filmy silk pullover than her nonexistent typing skills. During the interview, she had barely listened, so she had no idea what the office did. Only the note she had made on the back cover of Vogue recalled the address for her.

Receptionist. One of two. When she had interviewed for the job, the manager (Mr. Pauls? Mr. Peter?) introduced her to the present receptionist. From the look of the incumbent, the job consisted of flipping through a magazine, answering the mostly silent phone and greeting visitors who never appeared.

On Monday, Brandi pulled a pink LaCroix shirt from the recesses of her closet, pairing it with a Donna Karan skirt, ignoring the Delaurent separates that had been her earlier choice. The mirror refused her the invincibility reserved for the gods of retail. Receptionists were lesser creatures than salesgirls, she suddenly thought. Unworthy. Nothing she'd wear could return the power to her.

For a moment, she considered simply going to the store, punching in as if she had never left. The house account loomed large, however. Sighing, she headed for the new job.

At the last moment, she grabbed the shrug from the back of the kitchen chair, tugging its soft pink armor.

She took the bus two stops too far, then had to wait for one in the opposite direction. She couldn't remember when she was supposed to be at work. Neiman's opened at ten; maybe offices did too. To be on the safe side, she aimed at a nine-forty-five arrival, but the bus messed that up. It was eleven thirty when she appeared.

"She's here," snapped a heavyset woman sitting at the front desk. It took a moment for her to realize that the woman spoke into a tiny microphone. "You're late," the woman tossed the headset onto the desk then disappeared.

Brandi stared at the headset. Gingerly avoiding it, she settled into the seat behind the desk, pulling her shrug closer. Scrunching into the seat, she spun tentatively, right into a thin red head.

"Hi."

"Hi."

The red head stared until Brandi realized she was supposed to stand. "Sorry." Brandi stood awkwardly.

"S'okay. I was on break."

"The bus… "

"We can take turns, but somebody's gotta be here at eight. Tomorrow that's you."

Brandi found a chair pushed against the wall. Sitting, she gripped the seat tightly.

"Can you use a CP-30?"

"Uh…"

Not unkindly, the redhead asked. "It's Barbara, right?"

"Brandi."

"Says "Barbara" on your I. D." The redhead motioned at a card on the desk.

"Oh. Everyone calls me Brandi." Brandi picked up the card, which had a blank spot for a photograph.

"Alexis." She formed the word carefully. "Not Lexie or Al or anything like that."

"Alexis."

"You don't know the system. Come here."

Brandi pulled her chair closer.

"It's simple. When a call comes in, the button lights up. If it's the big one, then it's a call to the main line. One of the smaller buttons is a roll over - somebody didn't pick up their direct line."

They stared at the console for a moment. "When you pick up, say "Argent Metals, may I take a message."

"Argent Metals."

"Right. When I started, Mr. Mathews told me to say "May I help you" but I'm gonna take a message, so that's what I say."

"Take a message."

"Yeah. On the pad. Press hard, 'cause you have to make a copy."

"Why?"

Alexis stared at her. "Because you have to. It's the pad. Then you put the message in the rack." Miming, Alexis scribbled an invisible note, tore an invisible slip of paper and tucked it into a black plastic rack above the desk.

"That's it?"

"Sometimes someone wants directions or a phone number or something."

"I don't know the phone numbers."

"They're here." Alexis pulled out a ragged gray pamphlet. "If anyone asks."

They sat for a moment, looking at the console.

"Is there anything else?"

A few rules about breaks, eating at the desk, having messengers sign in. Nothing much. Brandi scribbled a few notes (at Alexis's urging) and stuck them on the phone. She was beginning to think that she and Alexis would never have an actual conversation when Alexis dropped her bag.

An explosion of cosmetics and papers littered the floor. Brandi hesitated, then helped Alexis retrieve her lipsticks.

And a large, plain post card.

"Sample Sale" read the card.

Beneath the plain type were incantations of holy names: LaCroix. BCBG. Fabrikant. Missoni.

Brandi gasped.

"What?"

"What is this?"

Alexis peered at the card. "A sample sale? You never been to one?"

Brandi shook her head.

Studying her critically, Alexis pursed her lips. "You a two?"

Brandi settled into her chair, hoping she passed Alexis's scrutiny. "Depends."

"Me, too. Most samples are six, maybe a four, but you can get 'em altered pretty cheap. You like Moschino?"

"Yeah."

"Okay. Here's the deal - these places, walk-ups? They have racks of clothes that were samples or maybe worn once, like a runway?"

"Yeah?"

"So they sell 'em - real cheap. You gotta look, some of it's faded and stuff, but most of it's great."

Brandi felt a glow in her chest. "Like half price?" she ventured hopefully.

"Half! No way - like a… a… tenth of what the stores charge."

"Where?"

"We're off at four-thirty. You can come with me."

At that moment the phone rang. At Alexis's nod, Brandi picked up the handset. "Argent Metals. May I h… May I take a message?"

It was a wrong number. Still, Brandi had passed the test. Small as it was, it felt like success. She slid the shrug down her shoulder, pulling the pink blouse.

"That's a great look," Alexis said approvingly.

"Thanks. It's a La Croix."

"I found a La Croix skirt on Thirty-First Street once. In a loft."

For the first time, Brandi looked at Alexis squarely. The red head wore a boring black sweater, over a fairly spectacular blue and red print shirt. "Bob Mackie?"

"Yeah! Wild, isn't it? You'll never guess the pants."

Alexis held out a slender purple calf. Brandi shook her head.

"I love capris, but I don't know that one."

"Laura Ashley."

"Get outta here!"

Conspiratorially, Alexis giggled. "Fortieth and Eighth. My mom wanted some sheets and crap - and these were there. Six bucks."

"For the sheets?"

"No, silly - for these!"

The rest of the day blurred. As four-thirty grew nearer, Brandi felt a ripple, possibly even a frisson. It was not the surge of power that brought invincibility, but the promise nevertheless.

Bio - D Ferrara

D Ferrara has been an active writer and ghost writer for more years than she cares to admit. Articles, essays and short stories are her continuing obsession – several publications, including *The Main Street Anthology – Crossing Lines, Green Prints, Amarillo Bay, The Penmen Review, The Law Studies Forum,* and *RIMS Magazine* have fed this mania by including them. Her short story, *Then and Now* was long listed in the Able Muse Write Prize for Fiction. *Arvin Lindemeyer Takes Canarsie* was a Top Finalist in the ASU Screenwriting Contest. Her play, *Favor,* won the New Jersey ACT award for Outstanding Production of an Original Play, while *Sister Edith's Mission,* and *Business Class* were produced at the Malibu Repertory Company's One Act Play Festival. Three of her full-length film scripts have been optioned.

She recently received her M.A. in Creative Writing, where it joined her J.D., L.l.M. and B.A, amid the clutter of her office.

East Meets West
American Writers Review

Honorable Mentions

Photo: Courtesy of Gerasimos Spathis

Nichole Kanney

The Bold and the Beautiful

Sugary-sweet scented air wafts down the production line as hundreds of worker bees build honeycombs like a well-oiled machine. The bees move along, carefully crafting each hexagon in a rhythmic pattern, as they've done many times before.

Secrete, shape, repeat. More worker bees follow behind, filling each new cell with a glob of partially dried amber nectar.

"Eighty percent water reduction on this batch. They're calling it some kind of designer pollen," one worker with black strips across her hindquarter, says to another identical bee.

"Only the best for Esmeralda," replies the other bee. A clear wax oozes from her underside. With her thin, black legs, she shapes the wax into a perfectly uniform hexagon.

Hundreds of bees buzz and zoom, constantly crafting, always depositing. A harmony of cooperation, a celebration of uniformity. The symphony of bees sustains the hive for the colony's greater good. Everyone doing as they're commanded.

Everyone except Beatrice.

Beatrice isn't your average honeybee. Of course, she *seems* average. Each day she works building comb cells just like the other girls. She's recently started this job, and isn't quite excelling at it, not like she did in her previous position. Back in the larval cells, all the nurse bees admired her because she produced the most potent royal jelly. Now she's stuck in this hot and humid factory making six-sided storage bins from her own body waste.

Beatrice is one of tens of thousands of bees. Just one of tens of thousands of bees conforming to a lifestyle that none of them chose - at least that's how she sees it. Day in and day out, working, working, working, and for what? Queen Bee Esmeralda? Well, who stopped copulating and made her queen?

A squeaky voice knocks Beatrice from her daydream. "Phoebe."

"What?" Beatrice asks, still dazed.

"She made Esmeralda queen." The worker taps her twig-like leg against the adjacent cell. Beatrice knew there was no time to waste. The glob in the worker's mouth needs a cell. And fast.

Beatrice pats all four of her legs to shape the partially set wax. It's misshapen and far from perfect, but it'll have to do. The worker bee deposits the glob of nectar in the cell.

"And by the way, those thoughts only lead to trouble. You'd be better focusing on your building skills." The worker bee flies away, antenna twisted in disapproval.

"Those thoughts only lead to trouble," Beatrice mocks. She crawls to an empty space, inhaling deeply. The soft fur on her back brims with moisture from the hot air. She calmly exhales. She secretes the next cell's wax. A tiny orange speck catches her eye. The nectar.

Beatrice shakes her head, ignoring it, and concentrates on building. With each one hundred and twenty degree angle she miters, the craving grows stronger. The orange bit teases, tempts. Just a little bit. Everyone's so wrapped up in their own work. No one will notice. She shapes a sidewall and struggles to maintain focus. She can taste the smell of it on her antennae. It's so sweet. She looks around. Hundreds of bees, hard at work, none paying attention to her. The gleaming pool of sugary bliss is only inches from her. Bart would love fresh nectar.

The pheromone-laden stench weakens; the workday's over. Bees finish up their current cells and the day's last deposits are sealed safely away. Beatrice's antenna shakes as she eyes the tempting succulence.

At home, Bart's lounging on a chaise made of wax. It's a modern honeycomb cell, but with very few amenities. It's precisely decorated to the likes of interior designer, Isaac Mizrabee.

Beatrice buzzes through the doorway, exhausted from her long day. The sticky pools from breakfast are still on the counter where Bart promised to clean. "Would it hurt you to get off your lazy bee-hind and do something around here?"

The sting of her purse punches Bart's abdomen, interrupting his relaxation. Bart pushes her purse away, and it falls with a thump. A bit of honeycomb rolls out to the wax-tiled floor.

"May I remind you that I have no means of self-protection? Venturing out now could kill me." Bart stands, stretching his wings. His eyes focus on the contraband. "What's that?"She flutters to the spilled purse, scoops up the questionable contents, and cinches the bag closed.

"Did you steal nectar? What were you thinking? Esmeralda will--"

"Everything we do, think, and say is about Esmeralda! I'm tired sick of it!" Beatrice's wings flap so violently, the fine-branched hairs on her thorax ripple like prairie grass in a storm. She buzzes a low ominous hum.

"That kind of talk's treason around here," he warns.

"Fine! Then I won't stay."

"Now, now." He closes in, making soothing motions with a segmented leg.

It doesn't work. Beatrice exposes her stinger.

"Whoa! There's no need for that," he pleas, pushing back with his middle legs. He retreats behind the chaise like the submissive drone he is.

Beatrice knows she upset him. "You're right. I over-reacted." Her silvery wings slow and she drifts to the kitchen area. She scoops two portions of stolen nectar into little wax bowls, then offers one to still-timid Bart.

"You know," she begins, "it's not such a crazy idea to leave the hive."

"Of course it's not." Bart nods, antenna vibrating with excitement. "Your time will come when you're all grown up and become a forager." He takes a bite of nectar. "And from the taste of it, quite a good forager, I must say."

Beatrice moans. "Right. Foraging for Esmeralda."

"Yes. For our wonderful queen, Esmeralda. I hope she'll pick me as a suitor when she embarks on her mating flight. "

"How can you call her wonderful?" Beatrice snaps. "It's because of her that I can't start my own family. She's a buzzkill."

Bart mumbles through a sticky mouthful. "But that's your destiny."

"Says who? Some stupid nurse bee who couldn't possibly produce royal jelly as good as mine? Who's *she* to determine my fate?"

His head lifts slowly from the bowl. "Where's this coming from? You took a huge risk stealing dinner. Relax and enjoy it."

She hasn't touched her bowl. Bart licks his bowl down to the rim.

"I want to go."

He stops mid-lick. "Go where?"

"Out," she answers. "I'm going to… to see the flowers."

His eyes widen. "But… You can't. You won't be able to come back."

She sighs, head lowered. "I know."

"You're just tired from work. Come on, sit down. Relax,"

"Don't you see? That's all I do. And for what? To be forced to steal my dinner?"

She grabs her purse and a saffron-fiber scarf from a hook near the door. She wraps it around her head. "Good luck, Bart. I'm outta here." She flies through the opening.

Bart's head twists, mandibles gaping, still holding the half-licked bowl.

She doesn't get far before she smells it. Pungent pheromones emanate from someone nearby. *Esmeralda*. The hive's on high alert.

Bart drops his nectar bowl, the smashing sound radiating through the comb cells like echoes in a cavern. Esmeralda and her entourage of drones shift their attention toward Bart's cell. She glides to his door, antennae quivering for closer inspection.

"Esmeralda, my lovely queen. What… what brings you here?" Bart asks, leg hair prickling.

Esmeralda towers over Bart. Her long skinny thorax flows behind her like a regal train. "Someone's been stealing nectar."

Beatrice hides around the corner of a nearby cell. She's close to the unguarded hive entrance. The guard bees are assisting Esmeralda in questioning the suspect. She looks back. Drones circle around Esmeralda, closing in on Bart. There's only one punishment for stealing nectar.

It's now or never.

Bart kicks the sticky bowl shards, complete with nectar remnants, under the chaise. "No nectar here. No stolen nectar, I mean." Bart is defenseless.

Beatrice eyes the exit again. She stretches her wings and cracks her knuckles. She's ready. She jumps off the piece of honeycomb and flies. She makes a sharp turn back toward Bart. The pheromones from Esmeralda are intoxicating. Her vision clouds. Wings flap all around her; the sound deafening.

A swarm.

She swoops in and lifts Bart by the abdomen.

"Let's go!"

At the junction between the entrance and the hive, a mound of sticky pollen threatens to rip Bart from her grasp. "Beatrice!"

She pulls him tighter to her thorax, collapses her wings, then zooms up and over, barrel rolling through the narrowing.

The swarm chases close behind the duo toward the exit. Beatrice has never felt so alive. She flaps harder and faster, her wings like miniature jetpacks thrusting her forward. Finally, the light. Beatrice throws Bart through the exit as a guard grabs her back leg. She reaches into her purse and finds one last glob of nectar. She throws it behind her, catching the swarm by surprise. The guard loosens his grip and she kicks him away. She soars out of the hive, into the bright blue freedom.

Nichole Kanney is a freelance copywriter, SEO consultant, and marketing assistant. She received her B.F.A in Screenwriting from the University of the Arts in Philadelphia, and has completed her M.A. and M.F.A. from Wilkes University. Her short script "Fridge Mates" has recently been selected as a quarterfinalist for the 2015 ScreenCraft Short Screenplay Contest. She currently resides in Richmond, Indiana with her husband, two children, four cats, and a plethora of fish.

Photo: Courtesy of Patricia Florio

Kayleigh Demace

Audrey

We've been in the car for hours. Nick is holding my hand as we pass a group of looters breaking into a CVS. Lila is still confused about what's going on, but luckily has fallen asleep for now. Thank God she's sleeping. This is the first group of looters we've passed so far, and will not be the last. Hopefully we get to the hotel soon.

This just in. The asteroid is still on course—. I shut the radio off quickly. Twice a day, every day, we get an update like this. We all know what's coming. A massive asteroid is due to hit Earth any day now. The government still hasn't released details, but the asteroid will be hitting in less than one month. After all this time the human race will cease to exist. Somehow, it hasn't gotten crazy yet. The looting just started a few weeks ago, but police forces in this part of the country say they are committed to keeping things as under control as possible. The president also gave an address soon after the discovery of the asteroid saying he believed we would all benefit from continuing to work, earn money, spend money, and operate normally. I'm extremely grateful for the small sense of normalcy they have established, especially since I've finally committed to finding my birth mother.

That's where we're heading now. I don't know how she'll respond when she sees me? I'm hoping it turns out for the best. What do I have to lose? The world could end tomorrow. I have tried to find her in the past but I would always talk myself out of it whenever I got close. I know her name, Anna, the city where she lives, Chicago, and how many dogs she has, two.

Just the other day, for about the billionth time since we first learned about the asteroid, I was looking through some old pictures of me and my adopted family. At the beach, on my birthdays, and at my wedding. I was always the odd one out. Even in the pictures, with us all laughing together, you can clearly see that I don't belong there— everyone leaning together naturally, and then me, standing just a little to the side, smiling. All of the girls in my adopted family are blonde, but my adopted father has jet black hair, only slightly speckled with grey in his old age. But me? I'm a redhead. It's darkened over the years, but there has never been any denying that I just did not belong with that family. My adopted father was the one person in my family who I could almost see myself in. As my hair darkened, and as he taught me how to take care of my car, I felt more and more connected to him. It's probably why I never longed to find my real father. I know nothing about him. Never really tried.

I had a great upbringing, but I have always wanted more. I wanted to see myself reflected in someone else. I wanted to know that I belonged with that person. I still want that now, but I also want Anna to see those pictures and know that the girl she had brought into the world had a great life and wasn't going to die unhappy. I need to know the same of her, too.

Luckily, the world isn't quite ending like it does in the movies. Sure, there are the looters, but the cars didn't all break down at once and the highways are still functioning normally. Chicago is only three states away from Pennsylvania, and the drive has been an easy one so far. I can't believe I'm finally doing this.

I told Nick everything for the first time yesterday. I was in the kitchen pouring myself wine when he pulled into the driveway after getting home from work. I was able hear the news update coming from his car. Based on what I heard, it sounded like we were running out of time. I never told him that I knew where she lived and had thought about finding her so many times before. And now, out of nowhere, I was going to ask him to leave his job. Or at least take a few weeks' vacation. They were all paid now anyway, since no one really had a future budget to worry about.

Lila was playing out back in a new playhouse we bought her. I yelled to Nick from the kitchen, where I was pouring him a glass of wine. Already armed with my own, I prepared myself to tell him about Anna.

"I'll tell ya what," he said, taking his Rolex off as he walked into the kitchen, "Thank God we're all still working. I'd go nuts sitting here all day waiting to die." I couldn't look away from my glass. He noticed right away that something was off and asked me what was wrong.

"Well," I hesitated for a moment. I knew he wouldn't deny me this, and the reality of everything was starting to set in. I was so nervous. Finally, I told him that I knew where my birthmother was.

He leaned onto the kitchen island and said, "Okay. Where is she?"

I told him everything. How I had easily found her through Facebook and was armed with this information for years. He listened silently, looking down and lightly kicking the base of the island. I waited a bit before asking him if he would leave his job to go with me. He looked up with a smile on his face and said, "For you, you know I would." I was a little worried that he would have a hard time understanding why I wanted to find her now, but he didn't.

He insisted on driving, too. Lila was restless the entire car ride after she woke up. She couldn't rap her head around why we were in a car for so long, which was our fault— my fault. I haven't told her much. Just that we were going to visit someone. I'm going to tell her everything in the morning. We finally reached the hotel. Both she and Nate fell asleep immediately, but I'm wide awake just looking at them. Every time I look at her like this I need to hold back tears. She's only nine years old. She's always been bright, always loved animals. She started talking about becoming a veterinarian about two months before we found out about the asteroid. Knowing that she'll never get a chance at life kills me. I can't help but wonder if Anna ever thinks about me this way.

***

We're at her door now. I can hear her dogs running around inside, birds singing their morning song outside. Lila reaches up to ring the doorbell. I explained everything to her this morning, and she took it very well. She nodded the entire time and asked no questions. Just as we pulled up to the house she said, "Mommy, I hope grandma likes us," and smiled. She knows about the asteroid, realizes what it means and how serious it is, and is still always so cheerful.

A man answers the door. He's wearing an open Hawaiian shirt, and looks to be about 50 years old… around the same age as Anna, if I'm not mistaken.

"Can I help you?"

"Yes, we'd like to see Anna, please," I say.

He nods as he turns around, yelling her name. Turning back to us, he gestures for us to come in.

"You can close the door behind you."

We do as he says and Nate takes my hand in his once again, interlacing our fingers. Lila is right in front of us, hugging her teddy bear and slightly bouncing on the balls of her feet.

Anna had been upstairs. As she descends the long, lavishly carved staircase, I notice that she has the same hair as me. Brown, but deep red when the sun hits it, and cut to her shoulders. She looks down at us and pauses for a moment.

"Audrey," she says with a smile. Tears start pouring down her face as she rushes down the stairs, stopping short right in front of us.

"Anna... you know me?"

"I'm so glad you're here. Is this your family?" I could only nod. "Please, come in so we can talk."

"I'm Bill, by the way," says the man in the Hawaiian shirt. "Anna's boyfriend."

Nick reaches out to shake his hand. "I'm Nick. This is my wife, Audrey, and our daughter, Lila." He has entered salesman mode, smiling and not the least bit uncomfortable.

"Please, come with me. Dinner will be done soon, you can stay. Lila, would you like some apple juice?"

"Yes, please, grandma," she says with a smile. With that, Anna and I are both a mess of tears and smiles. She takes my hand and leads us into the living room to sit down. Bill has gone to get Lila's juice.

"Your adopted mom was a friend of mine for years before I had you" she says, wiping away tears. "I was devastated when she passed away last year." We sit down and she pauses for a moment.

"I was messed up back then. Involved with all the wrong people. I needed to give you to someone I trusted, but I had to stay away."

"No, it's okay. We don't need to talk about it right now. I just… Are you happy?"

She hesitates briefly. "There was always an emptiness in my life," she says. "It's been really hard on me over the years. I wish I had reached out to you before. I should have when your father disappeared on me. But yes, I am. Bill has made me very happy. He would have dropped everything to take me to you, if I just hadn't been so scared," she says, looking over to him as he hands Lila her juice.

"Please," she says, pulling my attention back to her, "stay here with us. There's no use in you going back now, what with …" she trails off, not needing to finish her thought.

"I brought these for you," I say, pulling out the photographs. Tears form in her eyes once again and we begin to go through the pictures. Nate excuses himself to join Bill and Lila.

As we talk over the pictures we hear the news anchor interrupt a radio program with an important update:

Breaking news tonight: Scientists have confirmed that the asteroid will be hitting us tomorrow at approximately 8:37 am... That is all.

A timer goes off in the kitchen. Dinner is done.

Kayleigh DeMace lives in Wilkes-Barre, PA and works in book marketing. She holds a BA in professional writing and literature from King's College and is currently working towards an MA in creative writing from Wilkes University. Her favorite book is *Little Women,* likely due to her playing Marmee in a stage production years ago. This is her first published short story.

Photo: Courtesy of Kevin Freibott

Finalists

OUR LAST DANCE

Samantha Griffith

You offered your hand,
I declined.

But your voice.

Beautiful as ever.
Sweet with mirth.

We circled each other with
Delicious words caressing our thoughts
Evoking memories of cool breezes
Lacing warm summer nights filled
With laughter and music and friends.

You stirred memories.
Ones of warm breath on the nape of my neck,
Your hand caressing the small of my back.

Memories of our bodies pressed

As one as we danced,
Swaying
To the beat,
To the beat,
To the beat.

Swirling,
Laughing,
Whispers of heady words,
Planning,
Building hope of love and life.

How was I to know it was our last dance,
My last invitation.

But I should have known.

It was in your voice,
Your unsteady foot,
Insecure,
Unsure of the
next step.

You, who are always
So sure.
You, now lost
calling for our last dance.

I, lost in the memory
of our last dance
Declined.
Not from wanton malice
But from pride.

I never dreamed it was
my last chance to
dance,
entwine,
caress,
breathe in each other's breaths,
share in each other's smile,
Move
To the beat,
To the beat,
To the beat.

You offered your hand
I declined.

Without music nor movement,
Without smiles nor whispered thoughts,
Nor warm caressing breath,
You chose to stop dancing,
To slip away into the night.

What if I had not declined.

Photo: Courtesy of www.googlepics

Butterfly

Joel Heller

Have you ever lured a butterfly
To just within your reach?
She is elusive as a breezy gust
On her whim she may retreat.

If she rests upon your finger
To flash enticing looks,
One moment of her beauty
Can fill a poet's book.

Come, come my pretty butterfly
Bring your grace into my day,
Your presence will long linger
Though you'll inevitably ...

...fly away

Photo: Courtesy of Patricia Florio

Gary S. Crawford

Encounter

Long lonely desert highway. Boy, they weren't kidding. A car hasn't passed me for a good half hour. I saw one way behind me for a while, but I don't see him now. Where did everyone go? Oh, okay, I haven't been transported to an alien planet after all. Here comes a semi. Hey, Mr. Big Truck, good to see you. Like two ships passing in the night, two lonely drivers passing in the desert. He must be lonely too, as he waved to me before I waved back. Bye, Mr. Big Truck, have a safe trip, wherever it is you're going. Wow, the high point of this trip is being passed by a semi.

Just a dot in my mirror now. Wonder where he came from? Where he's going? I remember when I had a CB radio and could talk to those guys. A little chat to keep you going on a long trip.

Okay, three miles until I get to the world famous Desert Stop. Those signs have been counting off every mile for the last ten or twelve. Okay, world famous Desert Stop, you have my attention. Could use a bathroom break. Maybe a sandwich and a cup of coffee. The sign says gas, food, and snacks. Hell of a marketing plan.

I wonder if this place is like those middle-of-nowhere desert gas stations? Beat up old place, hasn't seen a coat of paint in twenty years, some old guy in overalls and a straw hat pumping your gas and telling you his life story. Home of the world's largest ball of pocket lint, world's largest kidney stone, biggest collection of two-headed snakes, some other off-the-wall claim to fame.

Yeah, right out of one of those American International movies from the 70s, Roget Corman directing, the second movie of a double feature at the drive-in. Biker movies like "Wild Angels" with Peter Fonda and Nancy Sinatra. Oh yeah, Nancy Sinatra. Ol' Blue Eyes sure could make pretty babies, couldn't he?

Two miles to go. I'm getting all excited now. Yeah, right. But it'll be nice to see other humans after this painfully long trip across no-man's-land. Pretty though, I have to give it that. Empty for miles in every direction, scrub plants scattered around. Every ten miles you might see a jack rabbit shoot across the road. That old abandoned trailer that somebody once lived in. Or maybe they still do. Those three junk cars together at the side of the road back there. Stripped of anything good on them, probably fifty years ago. Coming over that last rise, I could see a good five miles ahead, the road stretching straight across the desert.

One mile left. I think I see it. Shoot, with my luck, the place closed down years ago and just the signs remain. No, I see some cars there. Is it open? God, I hope so, with all the hype and ballyhoo of those signs every mile.

I think it's open. Hey, lights! I'll be damned! It's open! Yeah! Might as well gas up while I'm here, you never know how far the next slice of civilization might be. Prices aren't bad.

Long trip, that's for sure. My leg is asleep.

"Well, good afternoon to you too, sir. Beautiful day. Yes, fill it with regular. Cash. I need to use your rest room. Over there? Thanks."

Nice old guy. No overalls, though. Work pants and a tee shirt, no straw hat. Long gray hair in a ponytail and a beard. You'd expect different? Maybe he just said to hell with the rest of the world and bought this place way out here. I wouldn't mind something like that.

Let's see now. We need food. The sandwiches in this case all look fresh.

"What's that? Oh, made this morning. Thank you, ma'am."

Where did she come from?

Oh, look at that. An old Coke self-service case. I've got to have a Coke. Oh, even the old little bottles too, bottle opener on the side of the case. I loved these things. Ice cold Coca-Cola. So cold it hurt your throat on that first gulp. Thick glass on those little bottles, kept it nice and cold.

"Yes, ma'am, a sandwich and a Coke. Thank you. I think I'll sit outside at the picnic table and see if any cars go by. Not many, I can see that. But they all stop here? That's good for business, I guess."

"Okay, Mister, how much for the gas? Gee, that's not bad. I have exact change. Thank you too. I'll just move my car over there out of the way. You never know, another car might pull in."

I like his laugh. Probably a fun guy to have a beer with. Late fifties, I'd say, in good shape. The lady inside is probably his wife. Must have been a looker in her day. Still pretty nice.

Okay, let's park it at the table here. So quiet. I could get used to quiet like this.

But not for long. What's that? Way off in the distance. It sounds like a motorcycle. See? I told you this was right out of a Roger Corman movie! Here come the bikers!

It's getting closer. Sounds good. That isn't some off-the-showroom-floor stock Harley. Can't wait to see it. Still way off. Sound travels forever out here.

I think I see it. I see chrome shining in the sun. Closer now, it looks stretched out, like some custom chopper. Slowing down, I guess he's stopping here. Nice looking from what I can see so far. Yup, he's pulling in. And that ain't a he, that's a she!

Pulling up to the pumps now. Here comes the old dude. Hands her the nozzle, she puts it in the tank. And in just a minute she's done, just like that. Just topping off. Hands the guy her money and walks toward the building. Pushes her sunglasses up on her head. Will you look at that? She's gorgeous!

Sorry, doll, but I can't help but stare. Real women don't look like you. Wow.

Okay, shut up now, here she comes. You'll ruin everything by opening your mouth.

She smiles, says hello, calls me "fellow traveler" and asks if she can join me.

Think before you speak now. "Sure, have a seat."

There, got all that out without making a fool of myself.

Now, better to keep my thoughts inside. My dear, you are at least a twelve on a scale of ten. Tall, about 5'7", you are about 130 pounds, gorgeous. Early thirties. Long dark hair to your waist. So black it shines blue. And that skunk stripe of silver hair coming from your left temple running all the way to the end. Is that natural? Whatever it is, it looks fantastic. I wonder if you had those jeans tailored to fit you. Incredible. Tattoos on your upper arms. And that final man killer, the tight black tank top. It's a shame you have it all stretched out like that. A little cleavage, black bra strap peeking out, don't you know what this does to us guys? Yeah, you probably do.

God bless your Mom and Dad. Mmm!

"Where am I going? Oh, east."

She smiles. She's going west. Well, that was pretty obvious from the way she was going when she pulled in.

"Any place special? No?"

She has friends in Sacramento and she might head that way, but that's not where she's going.

"Just riding west. It must be nice to have the chance to do that. Just hop on your bike and ride."

Her pretty smile says that's how she likes it. Sparkling white teeth surrounded by her deliciously tanned coffee-with-cream complexion, and that awesome black hair with its silver skunk stripe. She can't be real. A desert mirage – yeah, that must be it.

"How was your coffee? That's good. Me, I'm going for another ice cold Coke. Yeah, they are pretty good. Just like the old days."

She asks me my name. It takes me a few seconds to remember it and tell her. Duh. I ask her for hers.

Raven. What a great name for someone who looks like her, especially with that stunning blue-black hair.

"Yeah, I guess we both have to be on our way. Nice to meet you too. Have a safe trip, Raven."

I walk her to her bike. Sweet machine. All metalflake purple and chrome. She gets on, adjusts her sunglasses, flips her long hair back over her shoulders, punches the start button.

Raven leans over and kisses me on the cheek. She smiles as she kicks it into gear and rides off, nailing it as she hits hard pavement, her hair blowing wildly.

All I can do is watch as she rides west, growing smaller and quieter as she fades from view.

Damn.

Bio – Gary S. Crawford

Gary S. Crawford is a Jersey Shore native and local historian, editor and award-winning author. He has published many articles on historical subjects, including the "Historical Vignettes" column in the *Asbury Park Press* and other local newspapers as well as several national magazines. Considered an authority on the Morro Castle ship disaster, he has published a companion book to his lecture series on the disaster. He co-authored the ARCADIA IMAGES OF AMERICA BRADLEY BEACH NJ. He has also published many short stories in several anthologies, three of them winning awards in the EAST MEETS WEST series. Crawford has published the horror novel VOICES OVER THE MOON and war veteran horror-fantasy VOICE OF A HERO, both available on Amazon and BN.com.

Crawford has a degree in business administration, minoring in creative writing. He lives at the Jersey Shore with his wife Dawn, their grown daughter Amy, and three grandchildren. Email: GSCauthor@gmail. com or web:
http://www.crawsat.wix.com/garyscrawford

or his blog: "Creative Bellyaching" at
http://garyscrawford.blogspot.com

Photo: Courtesy of Gerasimos Spathis

Uncanny X-men Issues 141 and 142

Brian Fanelli

When I read *X-men Days of Future Past*,
I clenched my covers, flipped through pages,
horror-struck that the team of superheroes died,
wiped out in a dystopian future by sentinels
that stalked alleyways, patrolled streets,
busted hideouts where the X-men made a last stand
against a robot army created by man
to destroy mutants because they were different.

When I read issues 141 and 142,
I wept when Storm was impaled,
Colossus was crushed, and even Wolverine
was pulverized by a sentinel's laser blast, reduced to skeleton.

For months I locked windows, bolted doors,
feared one of those robots would tower in my yard,
yank my family from our home late at night,
jail us in mutant concentration camps.

Now when I circle the park near my house,
overhear a bully drop the word fag,
or recall the graffited swastika scrubbed off
a nearby building, I remember how the sentinel's creators
spewed the word mutie again and again in speeches.

At least when I read the final pages,
I could go to sleep knowing
Kitty Pryde succeeded in going back in time
and preventing that awful future.
At least in the comics there's a way to revive
superheroes and stop bigots from imprisoning
or exterminating anyone different.

BIO: Brian Fanelli is the author of two books of poems, *Front Man* and *All That Remains*. His poetry, essays, and book reviews have been published or are forthcoming in *The Los Angeles Times*, *World Literature Today*, *Paterson Literary Review*, *Blue Collar Review*, *New York Quarterly*, *[PANK]*, and other publications. His poetry has also been a finalist for the Allen Ginsberg Poetry Prize and the Tillie Olsen Creative Writing Award. Brian has an M.F.A. from Wilkes University, teaches at Lackawanna College, and is a Ph.D. student at SUNY Binghamton.

The Gift
Carol MacAllister

After the rain,
long into dark spring,
on the bank of the River
Eight-Fingered Monk,
in the midst of a sloping,
cream-colored cloud
of wild flowers,
an old man's hands
flashed and gently
trapped a butterfly.

He held it aloft
fast in the light of
strengthening sun,
veined and translucent
Kallima, fluttering,
sweetly painted wings,
dressed as a falling leaf.

A warming sun froze
a diamond tear
in the corner of an ancient eye -
gnarled fingers parted,
the butterfly freed
floated soft among fragrant jasmine
kissed a white almond-blossom,
fluttered atop hedge rows
touched a quivering lotus heart,
then nestled amid
sap-tears of the giant pine.

Photo: Courtesy of Gerasimos Spathis

From the Editor's Desk
On Bridging the Gap

This past year of 2014 has been an interesting one. From the first day I set my foot into Wilkes University's Creative Writing Program in 2007 or '08 (now I can't remember) my mind has refused to shut down. It's a muse, I tell you, who keeps me up nights, throws me out of bed in the mornings and has me sitting on my living room steps writing in longhand first thing of the day. Or maybe that was Natalie Goldberg and Julia Cameron that inspired that chore. The writer inside me has been let out of its cage.

Because of the many states across America, and Puerto Rico, Carol MacAllister would chime in, I've become interested in bridging the gap. Of course, Facebook came up with its version first, and I don't want to take on that kind of a job. But having a distant writer share where they're from, what their state and town is like, that job I knew I could handle.

We started out with me sharing about my town in Ocean Grove, a sweet little Victorian Historic place by the ocean. Then Ginger wrote about her town in Alabama; how much she'd miss her mornings having a cup of coffee as she watched the world go by. Then Carol wrote about Puerto

Rico and its rain forest, the tropical surroundings that she experiences every day of her life.

Each edition of East Meets West American Writers Review will continue to include a place for writers to share their special place in our country. This time, we have Annastaysia Jade Savage who tells about her hometown of Waterford, Connecticut as well as the beautiful surrounding areas of New England.

East Meets West
American Writers Review

Bridging

the

Gap

A quiet stroll on Waterford Beach with her husband and dog Ace.

Photos: Courtesy of Annastasia Jade Savage

Annastaysia Jade Savage

I am an Abstract Expressionist artist and sometimes writer living and working in the New England shoreline town of Waterford, Connecticut. It's a quaint place located in New London county. It is situated cozily in between Mystic , of "Mystic Pizza" fame and Niantic, a small and quaint seaside village. You may have also heard of it because THE AMASTAD shores up in Mystic Seaport. The Eugene O'Neil Theatre might ring a bell as well, it's where many famous actors, like Michael Douglas, got their start. Or how about The Harkness Mansion and grounds? A beautiful seaside park. Whether you've heard of us or not, it's a place worth visiting, even if just for the seafood alone. Get the "Lobstah Roll".

The first thing I think of when I think of my home is the Atlantic Ocean and The Long Island Sound. The sea plays an important role here with many of Portuguese fisherman heritage residing in New London, our port town. We're called Waterford because we're surrounded on three sides by water, The Thames River, the Niantic River and Long Island Sound. You can easily take the ferry across the sound into New York. We're twelve miles from Orient Point in Long Island. While you're at it, take the Block Island ferry out and get lost on the isle with it's gorgeous beaches and picturesque main street for the day. We've got Pleasure Beach, Rocky Gap Beach, Ocean Beach, Niantic Beach, Hole in the Wall Beach, Waterford Beach, oh I could go on. All of these beaches are within 5-10 minutes from my house, from everyone in the community's home. I live at the end of the Niantic Bay, which is stunning year round. I eagerly await the arrival of the swan, geese and duck babies in the spring. I watch the American Bald Eagles dining on fish from the cove while sitting on blocks of ice with the seals in the winter. And you can't beat inlet kayaking in the summer. Fall, oh don't get me started on autumn. The world knows how beautiful New England Fall is already.

Don't like the water? You easily hit the mountains. Mohawk Mountain Ski and Ski Sundown are in Connecticut while we've got Ski Butternut and Catamount just over the New York and Massachusetts lines. (Remember, Connecticut can be driven across within 2-3 hours.) The mountains are great for what we call "Leafers", the city folk who come up from New York and New Jersey to view and enjoy our beautiful foliage in October and November when it's at its peak.

Are museums and culture more your thing? Try The Florence Griswold Museum, The Avery-Copp House, Blue Slope Country Museum, Captain Palmer House, The Children's Museum of Southeastern Connecticut, The Colchester Historical Society Museum, Cummings Art Galleries (part of the Art Center at Connecticut College), Custom House Maritime Museum, the Denison Pequotsepas Nature Center with live animals, the Dinosaur State Park and Arboretum, Fort Griswold Battlefield State Park and the Fort Trumball State Park, the Hempstead

Houses, the Lyman Allyn Art Museum, the Lyme Academy College of Fine Arts, the Mashantucket Pequot Museum and Research Center and you can't forget Mystic Seaport and the Mystic Aquarium. The aforementioned list is but a mere few of the cultural adventures you can have where I live. We have something for everyone, from Native American tribal culture to art museums, from aquariums to historic houses. And historic houses are amuck in Waterford. My home alone was built in 1650. We can even boast a haunted lighthouse at the converge of Long Island Sound and the Thames River. Go for the tour on Halloween if you can handle it. You won't be able to leave as it's completely surrounded by water. Here is the most up to date link for museums in Connecticut:

http://en.wikipedia.org/wiki/List_of_museums_in_Connecticut

Groton, another small quaint New England town next to ours boasts the Submarine Museum and the Coast Guard Academy. The museum is free to all. There's nothing more exciting than watching a submarine being towed in for repair while crossing the Thames on the Gold Star Bridge. It's almost as Majestic as watching The AMASTAD leave port.

Though I wasn't born and raised in Waterford, New London County, Connecticut, this is my home. Through our many travels and adventures, my husband was offered a position at the Groton Airport as a Helicopter Mechanic. After living on the side of a mountain for the past 4 years while he worked as a ranger, this was too exciting of an opportunity to pass up. So here we are, in a very special place we're proud to call home. We have all the art and culture we need, so my art business is thriving. We have the ocean and sound where we go crabbing and fishing for our dinner. We have bonfires in the evening while carving our pumpkins for Halloween. The people are friendly, not the "crusty old New Englanders" we were warned about. Just don't get upset if you're name is Anna and they call you "Anner". After traveling around the country, I've found this accent here to be so unique, they switch the a's and r's in their words.

Next time you find yourself on 95 North, get off on exit 75 and you'll have one adventure after another. Oh and don't forget - your "lobstah roll" will be free if you know how to dive for them.

Annastaysia Savage of AJ SavageArt is an artist and writer living and working in Waterford, Connecticut. She's currently completing her MFA in Painting and Illustration from The Academy of Art University and will be completing her MA in Creative Writing from Wilkes University in the Fall of 2015. You can find her latest publication, a young adult book titled *Any Witch Way*, on Amazon.com or BarnesandNoble.com You can view and/or purchase and commission her artwork here at: **www.ajsavageart.com** She lives in a house haunted by a ghost cat with her husband, their black lab Ace and two crazy "alive" cats. You can also find her on any one of Waterford's beaches when she leaves her studio.

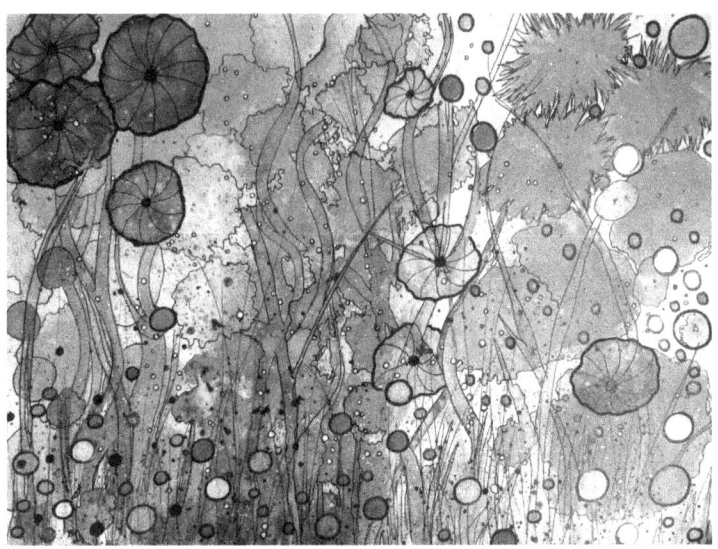

" Wonderland". Watercolors, Inks and Metallic on Arches Cold Pressed Paper. 16x20. 2014.

"Garden Magic." 30x40 Watercolors, Inks and Metallic on Arches Cold Pressed Paper. 2015.

East Meets West

American Writers Review

Book Excerpts

From our Staff

CONFESSIONS OF A COURT REPORTER

A Memoir-in-progress

By Patricia Florio

All our words are but crumbs that fall down from the feast of the mind."
- Kahlil Gibran

October 1985

Bankruptcy Court

I glance down to see if my fingers still hover over the home row keys of my steno machine. I type in the judge's name, date and time of my appearance in the courtroom. Court reporters don't usually look at their keys when they write. We mostly stare into space and trust our fingers to become our ears, keeping our minds at bay. In the three months that I've trained in this courtroom, I have learned to stop listening to the words, and just focus on the sounds of what others say. I'm a stenographic reporter, an alien from the planet I call "All Absorbed," just one of the many actors on the stage of life.

The field of court reporting is all about instinct, skill, and the many hours of practice that it took to this place inside the well of the courtroom, the common ground in front of a judge where attorneys stand alongside their clients. It is the center stage where judges sit up high peering down on those present, like wise old owls. They listen intently to the arguments presented. My ears and fingers listen, and tap out the sounds, the secret language that captures every word that flies in the air. The steno machine and I are one. If I start thinking about outlines and short forms, I can easily get flustered and freeze. I might even fall behind two sentences. And that is a no, no for a court reporter, even a new one like me.

Today is not practice. Today is not rehearsal. Today is the real deal, my first day on the job. I am nervous as anyone might be on their first day of work.

"It's okay to be nervous," Ron said sipping coffee at his desk earlier that morning, "that means you care." I had worked as Ron's transcriber, typing up transcripts for almost nine years prior to getting my court reporting degree.

The fact is, I really do care. I have these people's lives in my hands; their testimony flows through my fingers and it's important that I remain alert and concentrate. It's important that I don't screw up. But the anxiety in my head is deafening, all of the practice sessions in school play out over and over again. I take in a deep cleansing breath, having confidence in my capabilities. The machine tucked between my knees is my friend and my partner.

I look up to see attorneys gathering in the courtroom. They smile at me. I smile back.

"First day on your own, Pat?" Bob Musso asks as he approaches my desk handing me his business card. I shake my head affirmatively, rolling my eyes for effect. Bob's giant stature blocks out the light and casts a shadow over my desk.

"Don't worry, you'll be great. I'll speak slowly, I promise," Bob says grinning from ear to ear, as he rocks back and forth on one foot and then the other, something he seems to do even when he's presenting a case before the judge.

"Thank you," I say knowing I have one lawyer on my side. I staple Mr. Musso's business card on my copy of the judge's calendar.

As the courtroom begins to swell with attorneys and their clients, I wait until ten o'clock before I exit the back door to get into the secured corridor that takes me into the judge's his chamber. My leaving the courtroom signals the fact that the judge will be coming out to the courtroom: to sit up on that perch where he has a bird's eye view of *his* courtroom.

As I wait in chambers for the judge to don his black robe, I stand and converse with his secretary, Barbara. We exchange pleasantries, "Good morning or nice day." To our right, two law interns flip through pages beneath a tower of fifteen or twenty wooden shelves heavy with legal books. These books are among the issues of the Bankruptcy Code, the local rules, and West Law. They are bound in dark blue and graced with gold lettering across the front. Oftentimes, the judge refers to these tombs and cites passages from their pages. It is critical for me to pay attention to these legal cites, even though I'd be allowed to research the text and make copies of the laws governing particular cases.

While I wait, I begin to feel like Alice in Wonderland, a small and confused child dropped down a rabbit hole, now in the land of giant adults. My hands are trembling and my heart beats in unison. Ron's words reiterate in my mind, "It's okay to be nervous; that means you care."

Judge Feller steps from his private office, looks in my direction and says, "Let's go, Pat. It's show time." He walks behind me as I lead the way.

Although his face is stern, and he looks like a soldier marching to battle, I know he wants me to do well. He has selected me as his court reporter and I take comfort and pride in his decision.

He is right behind me as I rap on the back of the courtroom door, and shout, "All rise! Court's in session." I feel like I'm taking a friend into a surprise birthday party, when all of these people rise from their seats and stand up.

The judge walks up the three carpeted steps and takes his place in front of the bench. I stand in front of my machine, my hands at my sides, I feel better already. I get a sense inside my body that I'm going to be fine.

Before the judge sits in his black swiveled chair, he says, "Everybody may be seated." That's my signal to assume my position behind my machine. Act 1: My court reporting day begins.

******

SWEET TEA

Wendy Lynn Decker

Chapter One

Mama was different from other mothers, only I didn't realize *how* different, until the day she buried our Thanksgiving turkey in the front yard. At the time, Mama believed the sacrificial act would save our sinful souls. In actuality, it challenged me to sacrifice my own.

I'd been waiting around the house all day for the big feast. Mama had put the turkey in the oven early that morning, and it was near sundown. The smell of sausage balls and sweet potato pie lingered in the air making my mouth water and stomach growl. Luke, my twelve-year-old brother wore a face that told me if he didn't get fed soon, he might go hunting in the backwoods. But, he didn't say anything, which was very unlike him. My older sister, CeCe, didn't seem to care one way or the other. Like always, I nominated myself to find out what was going on. Like always, I discovered more than I bargained for.

"Mama, where's the turkey?" I said. "It's been in the oven all darn day. I'm starving."

She sprung up from the couch nearly knocking me off my feet. I jumped back.

"You wanna know where the turkey is, Olivia? I'll show you where the turkey is." She stormed out the front door and down the aluminum staircase, and stepped over the short picket fence into the tiny garden in front of our trailer home. She fell to her knees and ripped through the dirt and rose bushes with her bare hands. Strands of dark hair clung to her pale face. I watched in confused horror, shivering in the fear of not knowing what she was about to do.

She stood up, holding something in her arms. Grass and mud covered her clothes, smeared mascara darkened her high cheekbones, and the eyes of a stranger glared at me; a stranger I had met before. With outstretched arms, she stepped forward and shoved a fifteen-pound cooked turkey at me.

I backed away from the defiled bird. "It's okay, Mama, we don't need to eat turkey. . . . Heck, I don't even like turkey! CeCe, c'mere," I shouted.

My sixteen-year-old mind was used to what we called "Mama's quirks," but this was the worst yet.

I stood motionless. CeCe rushed to my side. Wide-eyed, she stared at Mama for a second and then spoke to her in a calm voice. "What's going on here, Mama? What are you doing with the turkey?"

"Tell her, Olivia, tell her!" Mama hollered as she dangled the bird by one hind leg at her side.

I couldn't tell CeCe if I wanted to because I hadn't a clue why Mama would bury our Thanksgiving turkey in the first place.

"I did it for us." She dropped the turkey onto the ground and started to cry. "We haven't been livin' right for the Lord, but now He will not forsake us."

She began a babbling chant. "*Jai . . . Guru . . . Deva . . . Om. Jai . . . Guru . . . Deva . . . Om.* Hold my hand, Olivia, say it with me . . . *Jai Guru Deva . . .*"

Leaving the turkey where she'd dropped it, CeCe took Mama's scratched and dirty hand and led her to the front door. Mama reached for mine with her other hand. I grabbed it and trailed behind.

"What's she saying?" I whispered.

"She's singing that John Lennon song Daddy used to play for her on guitar." CeCe gazed toward the sky and we chanted along with Mama as we led her into the house. "*Nothing's gonna change my world . . .*"

CeCe pressed on Mama's shoulders so she'd sit down, and I lifted a pillow from the couch and placed it behind her head.

My brother Luke peered at Mama with a narrow stare. "Where's the turkey, and when are we eatin'?"

"Just forget about the turkey," I hissed.

"I'm hungry." Luke yanked the refrigerator door open. He stared for a minute, and then slammed it shut. "Ain't never nothing in this house to eat."

Luke flew off into his bedroom, probably to dismantle his TV for the hundredth time. Daddy used to say Luke leaped out of Mama's womb and right into his toolbox. Daddy died in a car crash on December 8th. The same date Mama's beloved John Lennon was shot and killed. Daddy was the only man Mama loved more than John. It devastated her; it devastated all of us.

In a few weeks it would be the fourth anniversary of Daddy's death. The bizarre connection to John Lennon continued to twist Mama's mind and hinder our healing. It also sabotaged our holiday season.

Although we all suffered the loss of Daddy, I felt as if CeCe and Luke suffered the most. I was like the extra child on a wooden seesaw shifting from side-to-side; sometimes by Luke, other times by Mama. Splinters pricked me, wore me out, tempted me to hop off. I learned to pluck them with tweezers from God's first-aid kit.

"Don't worry, Luke, we'll eat turkey, just not right now," CeCe said, and pulled a glass from the cupboard. "I'll pour you some sweet tea, Mama. Tea always makes you feel good."

Mama sat quietly staring into space. Out of the corner of my eye, I saw CeCe grab a bottle of pills from the cupboard. She poured the tea into the glass and opened two capsules and slipped the contents into the glass and stirred.

"Here Mama, drink your tea." She held the glass to Mama's lips. She took a sip. After about four more sips, Mama placed the glass on the end table.

Not long after, she fell asleep.

"What did you do?" I whispered.

"I bought sleeping pills from the pharmacy. It won't hurt her. It'll just make her sleep for a while. She hasn't slept in days. Haven't you noticed?"

"I noticed," I said. "You think I don't hear her clanking dishes at the kitchen sink in the middle of the night, or blasting the TV while she watches those weirdo shows?"

Mama battled with sleep all the time. She slept either too much or too little. There was never an in-between with Mama in anything she did. Even when it came to God. Mama loved Him with all her heart or she wanted nothing to do with Him. We all followed suit with her decision to forget Him after Daddy died. However, lately, I found myself praying again. Mostly for Mama, that she would meet a nice man who'd take care of her. Then I wouldn't have to worry if CeCe left. The closer she came to graduating Landon Community College, the more frequent my prayers became.

CeCe grabbed her purse and sprinted for the front door.

"Where ya goin'?" I said. My heart quickened. I didn't want her to leave. What if Mama woke up and did something worse? She'd done many unusual things over the past few years, but this incident brought Mama's quirks to a new level of peculiarity. I followed CeCe outside to her car.

Go back inside," she said. "I'm just going to the store for some food."

She turned to get into the car, and I noticed a streak of dirt above her upper lip. I laughed. Sometimes I had to laugh after things settled down with Mama. Perhaps it was a nervous laugh, but it beat crying, and I had done enough of that after Daddy died.

"What in the world are you laughing at?" CeCe asked, annoyed.

"Hold still." I stretched the sleeve of my sweatshirt over my thumb and wiped away her dirt mustache. "You can't go anywhere like that."

She bent down and checked her face in the car's side mirror then pointed toward the garden. "Throw that turkey in the trash, will ya?" She took off.

Back inside, Luke stared at the TV.

"Where'd she go?" he whispered.

I reached inside my pocket and pulled out a piece of bubblegum. "Here," I tossed it to him. "She went to get some food, it's gonna be all right," I told him, although I had no idea if it would be.

Mama still lay asleep on the couch. Her deep breaths turned into heavy snores. She looked helpless. Not like a mother. Like someone who needed a mother, and seeing her that way filled my loneliness with more invisible pain.

After Daddy's death, CeCe and I accepted Mama's depression as natural. But weeks turned into months, and months into years, and it seemed as if Mama's grief transformed itself into another being who took up residence inside of her head. I never knew which one I'd be seeing from day-to-day.

The Button Legacy
Emily's Inheritence

Ginger Marcinkowski

Chapter 13

1960

The warm breeze of an unusual New Brunswick summer sent the sheer white curtains in the Polks' home fluttering, the fabric lifting and falling with the wind's rhythm. Ellen was hanging newly scrubbed sheets on the clothesline beside the house, a spot where the sun rising over the Tobique River would shine all day long. From his rocker, John heard his wife humming "In the Garden," her favorite hymn. The gentle lull of her voice had John's head bobbing toward his chest and then jerking upright as he caught himself snoring. Saturday afternoons were always peaceful. Carol might stop by before dinnertime with his grandson, Peter. From time to time, Maureen would arrive with the other grandchildren for Sunday dinner, although the sixty-mile journey often kept her away until the longer holiday weekends.

A small sewing bee was planned for the afternoon with neighbors Laura Cogswell, Mrs. Belcamp, and Mrs. Park all gathering to quilt a covering for the latest church arrival. John knew his quiet wife loved those moments of fellowship with her loud and boisterous friends. Although she would often sit silently among them, he could see that the women admired his wife and her ladylike ways.

A long, almost solemn creak interrupted John's lazy thoughts. The quick slam of the screen door sharpened him to attention. "John," Ellen said, the empty laundry basket hugging her left hip. "Do I have something on the back of my dress?"

She twirled around, the skirt of her cotton dress lifting slightly. John loved her simple beauty, the way her blonde-white hair sat braided on top of her hair like a German pastry. God had indeed blessed him with a good woman. "Come closer, dear," John said, craning his neck. "Let me see."

"John, I feel something," she said, twisting her neck left and right, brushing her hands over her backside. Her voice began to pitch an octave higher. "It's moving, I swear!"
"Well, stand still a minute." John rose from his rocker, placing his Bible on the kitchen table.

"It's there, John! It's there!" A moment later, her arms were swishing at her skirt, her body circling as though she were a dog chasing her tail.

John had little time to respond, with his wife dashing around the kitchen. "Slow down, Ellen, and let me get a look." John grabbed his wife's arm and spun her around just in time to see a field mouse disappear under her dress.

Ellen's scream was long and loud, decibels above any noise he'd ever heard her sing. In one swift moment, Ellen had rushed out the kitchen entry, flinging the screen door open and allowing it to slam in John's face as he followed. John watched her as she twisted and twirled, jerking her skirt from her body, big white buttons popping from the dress and skittering across the yard.

A grin began to cross his lips, as soft as a gentle sunset. His wife stood panting in the dirt driveway. Her dress was lying six feet from her, the mouse now long gone in terror. She was covered with a sheer white slip and nothing more. Her hair had fallen to her shoulders, disheveled, with bobby pins protruding from what was left of her braid.

"Don't you laugh at me, John Polk!" she said, bending to collect what was left of her clothing.
"Ellen?" Neither John nor Ellen had seen their guests appear from the path behind the house. Mrs. Park, Laura Cogswell, and Mrs. Belcamp stood, mouths agape, with their arms full of quilting swatches.

Ellen's eyes darted between her husband and her friends. John watched a look of horror creep over his shy wife's face. *God help her.* She took a deep breath and, without so much as an explanation, squatted to pick up her clothes and moved toward the kitchen door. "Come on, ladies!" Ellen spoke over her shoulder.

"We've got God's work to do."

The women first eyed John and then each other, shrugged their shoulders, and followed her into the house. A glint of sunlight bouncing off something white caught John's eye. He moved toward it, bending to retrieve one of Ellen's dress buttons from between the blades of the unshaven lawn. He held it to the sky and smiled.

By the time he returned to the kitchen, Ellen had dressed and was busy serving coffee and fresh rolls to her guests. She had always been a server, a reminder to him of the biblical Martha. Good and gracious. Their eyes met—hers signaling a warning, his playful. He walked past her to the oak hutch and reached for the tin box that perched there. Even though Ellen was not facing him, he could see her back straighten as the button dropped in, clamping yet another story inside.

East Meets West

American Writers Review

<u>*Staff*</u>

Photo: Courtesy of Gerasimos Spathis

Ginger Marcinkowski

Ginger Marcinkowski is the author of newly released, THE BUTTON LEGACY: EMILY'S INHERITANCE, and widely acclaimed, *RUN, RIVER CURRENTS*. She is an MFA graduate of Wilkes University and was a presenter at the 2014 Hampton Roads Writer's Conference. She has judged the prestigious ACFW Genesis and Carol Awards and has been a reader for the James Jones First Novel Award. She currently writes a monthly column for Book Fun Magazine who boasts over 400,000 subscribers.

Email: grm55@yahoo.com
Facebook Author Page:
https://www.facebook.com/writer.Ginger.Marcinkowski/info
Website: http://www.gingermarcinkowski.com/about.html
Blog: http://gingermarcinkowski.wordpress.com/blog/

Carol MacAllister

Carol MacAllister serves as judge for the National Federation of State Poetry Societies, and the Bram Stoker Award in poetry. MacAllister holds an MFA in Creative Writing with a concentration in both poetry and fiction. Her poetry is widely published, has won numerous awards and competitions, and has been presented in public venues. MacAllister has edited and published four collections of poetry of others' works. In addition, THE BLACKMOOR TALES, a short story collection is published by NHP as an E-novel, and MAYAN CALENDAR REVEAL.

Anne B. Henry

Anne B. Henry earned a M.F.A. in Creative Writing from Wilkes University in January 2011. She is currently conducting a creative writing workshop for adults in a continuing education program and runs writing workshops for teens. At the 2014 Woodstock Writers Festival, Anne was first runner-up in the Story Slam. Anne is a reader for the on-line literary magazine, *Hippocampus*. As she searches for an agent for her memoir, she is also hard at work on her novel, **TRUTH BE TOLD**, and a collection of character driven short stories.

Patricia Florio

Patricia Florio was a finalist in the Norman Mailer Fellowship contest in 2012. She received a Master's Degree in Creative Nonfiction and an M.F.A. in Creative Writing from Wilkes University. She is the author of two memoirs: **MY TWO MOTHERS**. *The second edition* of *My Two Mothers* includes recipes. Her latest book, **CUCINA AMELIA**, contains *Family Stories with Sicilian and Neapolitan Recipes* and is now available on Amazon.com. She has published several short stories; all featured on Amazon.com, one is a featured story in *All in the Game;* she received second place for her nonfiction story *Theresa* in Allthingsifmagazine. *Golden Boy* was published by Queens Literary, summer of 2013. http://www.patriciaflorio.com

Wendy Decker

Wendy Lynn Decker is the author of SWEET TEA: A Novel, which received an endorsement from National Alliance of Mental Illness (Middlesex County, NJ) in 2014. The fall 2015 edition will include a study guide. **THE BEDAZZLING BOWL**, an inspirational chapter book for young readers, received the Outstanding Read Award from FaithWriters Magazine. Her short stories appear **in CUP OF COMFORT Anthology, LETTERS TO MY MOTHER (Adams Media).** She also spent a year as a columnist for the online magazine, "**Sisters in the Lord, 'Highlighting Their Services'.**" She lives on the Jersey Shore and is working on a M.A/M.F.A. in Creative Writing at Wilkes University. http://www.wendylynndeckerauthor.com Her books can be purchased at Amazon.com or ordered at any bookstore.

Books by Our Staff and Judges

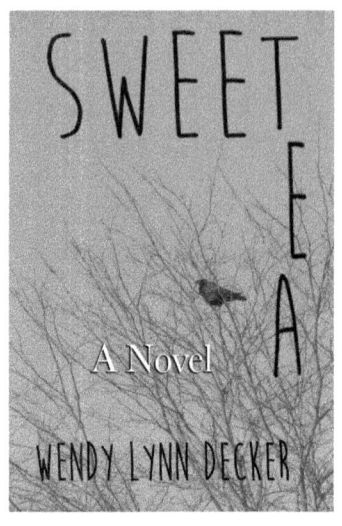

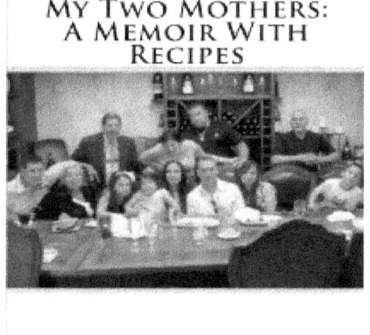

www.ingramcontent.com/pod-product-compliance
Lightning Source LLC
Chambersburg PA
CBHW072010170626
46813CB00005B/2091